3/93

D0820621

JOHN H. JOHNSON

"The Man from "Ebony"

Lucille Falkof

GEC **GARRETT EDUCATIONAL CORPORATION**

Cover: *John H. Johnson.* (UPI/Bettmann Newsphotos.)

Manufactured in the United States of America

Edited and produced by Synthegraphics Corporation

Library of Congress Cataloging in Publication Data

Falkof, Lucille, 1924-
    John H. Johnson, "the man from Ebony" / Lucille Falkof.
        p. cm. — (Wizards of business)
    Includes index.
    Summary: A biography of the black entrepreneur whose publishing company began Negro Digest, Ebony, and Jet, and whose other involvements in radio and in cosmetics have made him one of the four hundred richest Americans.
    ISBN 1-56074-018-3
    1. Johnson, John H. (John Harold), 1918-   —Juvenile literature.
2. Publishers and publishing—United States—Biography—Juvenile literature.   3. Afro-American periodicals—Publishing—History—Juvenile literature.   4. Ebony—History—Juvenile literature.
[1 Johnson, John H. (John Harold), 1918-   . 2. Publishers and publishing.   3. Afro-Americans—Biography.]   I. Title.   II. Series.
Z473.J75F34   1992
070.5'092—dc20   91-32775
[B]   CIP
                                                                 AC

Contents

Chronology for *John H. Johnson*

1918	Born in Arkansas City, Arkansas, on January 19
1933	Moved to Chicago, Illinois, to attend high school
1936	Graduation speaker at Wendell Phillips High School; went to work for Supreme Liberty Life Insurance Company
1941	Married Eunice Walker on June 21
1942	Began publication of first magazine, *Negro Digest*
1945	*Ebony* magazine first published in November
1947	Zenith Corporation became large advertiser in *Ebony*, other white corporations follow
1951	Received first national award as one of the country's Ten Outstanding Young Men by U.S. Chamber of Commerce; *Jet* magazine introduced
1957	Attended Ghana's independence celebration as part of U.S. delegation
1960s	Johnson Publishing Company became a spokesman for the black Civil Rights movement
1973	Bought first radio station, WJPC
1974	Founded Fashion Fair Cosmetics Corporation
1975	Harvard University celebrated John H. Johnson Day
1982	Named by *Forbes* magazine to list of 400 richest Americans
1984	Johnson Publishing Company became top black-owned business in the United States

Chapter 1

"Where Is the Man from Ebony?"

Incredible! That had to be the feeling that John Johnson experienced as he flew with Vice-President Richard Nixon to celebrate the independence of the new African state, Ghana. It was March 1957. One hundred fifty to two hundred years earlier, Johnson's ancestors had arrived in the United States as slaves from Africa. And only fifteen years earlier, he had been writing articles for an insurance company for twenty-five dollars a week. Now, here he was, having been asked by the President of the United States, Dwight D. Eisenhower, to be part of the U.S. delegation to the new African country.

As the Independence Day ceremonies progressed, Johnson could not help but be impressed that Ghana's head of state, Kwame Nkrumah, as well as the supreme court justice and the attorney general were black men running their own black country. Nor would he ever forget a Ghanian saying to him, "We Africans have our freedom. When are you Negroes going to get yours?"

Johnson and other black Americans went home fired up to do something. Among those blacks in the American delegation was one who was already taking action, Dr. Martin Luther King, Jr. It was the first time that these two historically important black men met. It would not be the last.

MEETING A BLACK EMPEROR

The trip to Africa included a visit to Ethiopia, one of the world's oldest countries. The delegation was invited to the royal palace of the emperor, Haile Selassie, the Conquering Lion of Judah. But with reporters and officials pushing their way to the front, it was difficult for Johnson to get a glimpse of the emperor seated on his throne.

Suddenly the emperor rose, looked over the crowd, and called out, "Where is the man from *Ebony?*"

Johnson could hardly believe his ears, but he raised his hand and was promptly escorted to the front. The emperor was a small but regal man, flanked by a pair of lions. Johnson noted happily that they were held securely by two strong men.

On approaching the throne, the emperor began explaining why he had called for Johnson. The emperor was an enthusiastic reader of *Ebony* magazine, but he did not always get his copies. Sometimes they were delayed or lost. John Johnson, publisher of *Ebony,* assured Haile Selassie that there would be no trouble in the future. Later, copies of the magazine were sent to the Ethiopian embassy in Washington and were delivered by special courier directly to the Lion of Judah.

In 1959, as a member of the press, Johnson would accompany Vice-President Nixon to Poland and Russia. He would be on hand to see the famous argument between the Vice-President and the Russian leader, Nikita Khrushchev. Johnson would also be wooed by Presidents and presidential candidates, who hoped to gain his magazine's support. He would feel at ease dining in the White House and throwing extravagant parties to celebrate the anniversaries of his magazines. "The man from *Ebony*" has made his mark on the American scene.

Chapter 2

Roots and the River

John Johnson's grandparents were the third generation born *after* slavery. But the heritage of slavery would linger down to the third generation. When "Johnny" Johnson was born in Arkansas City, Arkansas, on January 19, 1918, his home was a tin-roofed house three blocks from the Arkansas River. ("Johnny" was his given name. "John" would come later, when a more formal name was needed.)

His parents were Gertrude and Leroy Johnson. Leroy was a sawmill worker, a tall handsome man with a beautiful black mustache. (His son would also wear such a mustache when he became older.) But it was tiny Gertrude Jenkins Johnson who ran their home.

Though she had attended school only to the third grade, Gertrude was a strong and dignified woman, and she was a survivor. She survived an unhappy earlier marriage and the death of her husband, Leroy, in a sawmill accident when Johnny was eight years old. And she and Johnny together survived the great flood of April 1927, which President Herbert Hoover would call the "greatest peacetime disaster in [American] history."

THE GREAT FLOOD

"Run for your lives!"

That was one of Johnny's earliest and most vivid memories. One minute the streets of Arkansas City were dry and dusty. Within moments, the Arkansas River was spilling over its banks and rushing through the countryside, sweeping everything in its way into the muddy waters – mules, chickens, and homes. To Gertrude Johnson and her nine-year-old son, there was only one possible safe place. That would be the levee, a high island of ground surrounded by sandbags.

Grabbing Johnny by the arm, Gertrude raced toward the high land. Strong arms, both white and black, grabbed mother and son and frantically pulled the two of them to safety. John Johnson never forgot it was the American Red Cross that rushed food, tents, and other supplies to the worried whites and blacks. In his autobiography, *Succeeding Against the Odds*, Johnson describes this experience.

For six weeks, Gertrude and Johnny survived amid the crowd of people jammed onto the small island. They worried about the water snakes that slithered around them. They also worried that the sandbags might not hold. Then, when the wa-

The raging flood waters of the Arkansas River, from which Johnny Johnson and his mother barely escaped with their lives in 1927. (Library of Congress.)

ter finally receded, their worst fears were realized. They discovered that their little house was filled with mud. Gertrude and Johnny Johnson would have to start all over.

KEYS TO SURVIVAL

Hard work was the key to survival, and both mother and son once more put forth their very best effort. Gertrude worked as a domestic, cooking and cleaning for the white folks in town. Johnny would tag along, and he learned how to cook as well as wash and iron clothes. Johnny never saw himself as really "poor." Though their house was simple and lacked an indoor toilet, he always had enough food and good hand-me-down clothes and shoes provided by the people for whom Gertrude worked.

They were helped greatly when the year after the flood, Gertrude married James Williams. He turned out to be a kind and good stepfather to young Johnny.

The Church and Education

Hard work alone was not enough for Gertrude. She struggled to raise her son as a "good" person, one who attended church regularly and did not drink or develop other bad habits. When necessary, she did not hesitate to use a switch on her beloved Johnny. But she also was lavish with her hugs, and she had high hopes for her son.

Johnny was going to get the best education possible. Gertrude had a daughter, Beulah, from her first marriage who was fourteen years older than Johnny. Gertrude had made sure that Beulah received an education at the Arkansas City Colored School, and now Beulah was teaching at a school for blacks in a neighboring town.

The Arkansas City Colored School was run by C.S. Johnson, a graduate of what is today one of the best black colleges in the country – Morehouse College in Atlanta, Georgia. Though it was only a four-room schoolhouse, Professor Johnson and his wife, also a college graduate, set high standards for their students. They expected everything from neat clothes and polished shoes to good behavior *and* excellent grades.

The only problem with the school was that it just went to the eighth grade. There were boarding schools for blacks in Pine Bluff and Little Rock, Arkansas, but there was no way that a black could get a high school education in Arkansas City.

Johnny had managed to live with the fact that blacks

were treated different from whites in the South. He had learned to sit in the balcony reserved for black viewers when he went to the movies. He even learned to ignore the ugly word "Nigger!" occasionally hurled at him.

THE GREAT DEPRESSION

By the time that Johnny was ready for high school, the United States was suffering from the greatest **depression** the country had ever known. (Terms in **boldface type** are defined in the Glossary at the back of the book.) Millions of people were out of work. Without a job, many could not pay the **interest** on their **mortgages** and were losing their homes. Thousands of Americans were leaving their hometowns in search of work elsewhere in the country.

But Gertrude and her son were not about to give up on their dream of an education for Johnny. Instead of bemoaning their condition of being black and being too poor to afford boarding school, they looked at the choices they had. They could either remain in Arkansas City or they could go elsewhere. The question they asked themselves was, "What can *we* do to make things better for ourselves?" That question has become a part of John Johnson's basic creed, or set of beliefs.

According to a Chicago newspaper for blacks, called the *Chicago Defender,* and letters from friends up North, there were high schools and there were jobs for blacks in Chicago. Moreover, Gertrude had a childhood friend in Chicago by the name of Mamie Johnson. Mamie was married to a black railroad man (considered high-class work at the time), and they owned a three-story apartment building. Here was a place where Gertrude and Johnny could stay until they found jobs and their own apartment. Having this opportunity to improve their lot, they picked up the challenge. In John Johnson's own words, "We changed our fate and made a ladder out of a wall."

On to Chicago

But when Johnny graduated eighth grade at the Arkansas City Colored School, there wasn't enough money in the secret hiding place under Gertrude's mattress to get to Chicago. She thereupon decided that every member of the family would take every extra job he or she could find until they had the necessary funds. And Johnny would repeat eighth grade! Gertrude was not about to have her son running around town without something to do.

"You're going to stay in eighth grade," she said, "until we've got enough money to go to Chicago."

Fortunately, by July 1933, the family finally had saved the money needed for the journey. But Johnny's stepfather refused to go with them. He was sure that his wife and stepson would not find work and that they would freeze to death in the bitter Chicago winter. Gertrude loved her husband, but she was not about to sacrifice her dream.

On a steaming hot day, clutching fried chicken, potato salad, and marble cake in a brown paper bag, Gertrude and her fifteen-year-old son boarded the "blacks only" railroad car that would take them to Little Rock, Memphis, St. Louis, and – Chicago.

Chapter 3

The Promised Land: Chicago

When Gertrude and Johnny walked out of the Illinois Central Station in Chicago late that July night, they were overwhelmed by the sights. They had never seen such tall buildings, so much traffic, and so many black people. They had not realized how many blacks had moved north in the early 1900s.

The number of blacks in Chicago had increased from 44,103 in 1900 to 233,903 in 1930. During this period, millions of immigrants streamed into the East Coast from Eastern Europe. At the same time, millions of southern blacks moved north to such cities as New York, Detroit, Pittsburgh, Gary, and Philadelphia. Among the things they brought with them was a new music – the sounds of jazz, blues, and gospel (religious) music.

Though the blacks spoke English, they faced many of the same problems that the European immigrants faced – finding suitable housing and meeting **prejudice** because they were "different." The issue of color would be a barrier to blacks for years to come.

SETTLING IN

Settling into their new environment was made ever so much easier because of the kindness of Mamie Johnson and Johnny's stepsister, Beulah. Mamie had prepared an attic room for Gertrude and her son. Johnny was most impressed with the inside toilet and the fact that the house had steam heat for the winter months.

Beulah had left teaching and had learned dressmaking. She had been in Chicago for some time and had obtained a job in the city's garment industry. It did not take Gertrude long to find a job as a housekeeper, earning three or four dollars a day. That enabled Johnny and his mother to move to a rented room in the same building in which Beulah lived. The next step was to enroll Johnny in high school.

Life at Wendell Phillips High

With shoes scrubbed and polished, Johnny tried to appear "cool" as he faced the crowd of students milling around the registration desk at Wendell Phillips High School. But the number of students in the school was greater than the total population of Arkansas City.

Johnny could hear students calling out "1A" or "2B," but he didn't have the faintest idea what the numbers and letters meant. Not wanting to appear dumb, he called out "2." To his amazement, Johnny discovered he was enrolled in the tenth grade, the second year of high school.

Johnny could not help but enjoy the joke. He was probably the only student at Phillips High who had two eighth-grade diplomas, and now he was in the exact grade he should have been. Despite the loss of that ninth-grade year, Johnny quickly began to make his and his mother's dream come true.

Bit by the Journalism Bug

Johnny had always wanted to be a writer, to work on a newspaper, so he enrolled in civics classes to learn more about government and the rights and duties of citizens. He also took a journalism course and signed up to work on the school newspaper.

By the time he was a senior, Johnny Johnson was editor-in-chief of the school paper and sales manager for the school yearbook. The skills he learned in both writing and selling would be of tremendous value to him for the rest of his life.

More important were the models Johnny found at high school. For the first time, he saw well-educated and well-dressed black teachers who were respected and who respected their students. His teachers had a strong belief that their students could do anything on which they set their minds. He also had a wonderful white civics teacher, Mary J. Herrick, who taught her students about politics in Washington and London – and in Chicago.

Johnny's new hometown was a great place to observe politics. Black politicians and businessmen had been active in Chicago ever since the founding of the city by a black settler, Jean Baptiste du Sable. The Potawatomi Indians used to say, "The first white man to settle in Checagou was a black man."

Black businessmen had been quite successful in Chicago. It was here that the first black bank in America was established. Blacks also organized an insurance company and a cosmetics company, among other enterprises. Johnny was determined to move up in that company of black leaders, but the going was not easy.

DARK DAYS

As an "outsider" from the South, Johnny arrived at Wendell Phillips High with a thick southern accent and wearing "mammy-made clothes." He was very self-conscious about these differences, especially when his fellow students made fun of them. One day, after such an incident, he came home crying. At the time Gertrude was working for a woman whose husband was about the same size as Johnny. Gertrude was not too proud to ask for some old suits, and overnight, Johnny became one of the best-dressed young men in school.

Among his many activities, Johnny also took on the task of improving his speech. And he read books on self-improvement such as *Think and Grow Rich* and *How to Win Friends and Influence People.* By the time he graduated high school, he was a poised and capable public speaker.

Within a few months of their arrival in Chicago, Gertrude and her two children were able to afford a four-room apartment that cost thirty-five dollars a month. Beulah and Gertrude slept in the bedroom while Johnny slept on a rollaway couch in the dining room. (This was not an uncommon arrangement. Like many other children in those days, Johnny never had a room of his own until he was married.)

Shortly after, Johnny's stepfather, James Williams, moved to Chicago. It was at this time that life took a drastic downturn. Gertrude lost her job as a housekeeper and a little later, Beulah also lost hers. Even though James had predicted that the move to Chicago would be a big mistake, Gertrude could not blame him for what happened to the family. The truth was that from 1932 to 1935, the **economy** of the country grew worse and worse. By 1935, almost half of the blacks in Chicago were unemployed and on **relief.**

"On relief!" The very words made the proud family cringe. In desperation, they tried whatever measures they could to survive the crisis. Beulah left home to join a religious movement led by a black minister. Gertrude began to rent the one bedroom for five dollars a week, preferably to single men who did not want to use the kitchen or entertain in their room. This helped a bit, but it did not provide enough for food on the table and other necessities. There was no other alternative but to go "on relief," to seek help from the government. But when Gertrude applied, she was turned down because the family had not been living in Chicago long enough to qualify.

Gertrude Takes Command

Gertrude was not willing to accept the fact that her relief application had been turned down. There was one person to whom she could still make her appeal – the President of the United States, Franklin Delano Roosevelt. And she did! She sat down and wrote a letter to the President explaining the family's situation. Before long, she received word that the local relief agency would accept her application.

Roosevelt himself may never have read Gertrude's letter, but someone in his organization did. And this kind of caring impressed the family greatly. From being a long-time Republican, like most blacks, Gertrude became an ardent Democrat.

For two years the family remained on relief. The relief did not come in the form of checks, as it does today, but rather in foodstuffs. A government truck would roll into a neighborhood and deliver beans, salt pork, peas, and other items to a family on relief. As the truck approached, the young people sitting on the stoops of the apartment buildings would pretend that the delivery was not for their family.

Later, James Williams was able to get a job with the Works Project Administration (WPA), a federal agency (from 1935-1943) that provided public work projects to help relieve national unemployment. Johnny was fortunate enough to get a job with the National Youth Administration (NYA), a federal organization formed during the Great Depression to make work for young people. Now that both James and Johnny were employed, the family was able to get off the relief rolls. These government work programs enabled James, Johnny, and others to move into better jobs when the economy improved.

Despite the feelings of shame, John Johnson, as a grown man, would remember how important government relief, or welfare, was to the survival of his family and others. Even today, he encourages government programs that offer work to people as a step towards working in private industry.

A NEW LIFE BEGINS

By graduation day, there was no question in anyone's mind that Johnny Johnson was destined to become someone important. He was senior class president, had a scholarship to the University of Chicago, and was to be the only student speaker at the graduation ceremony.

Just before graduation two incidents occurred that affected Johnny's later life. His civics teacher, Miss Herrick, drew him aside one day and said, "Johnny, you're a big boy now. Shouldn't you be John?" It did not take long for the young man to realize the wisdom of her suggestion. He also took her suggestion to select a middle name and decided, for no particular reason, to choose Harold. His new name headlined an announcement of the graduation ceremony published in the school newspaper.

The second event happened at a luncheon for black honor students. The main speaker at the luncheon was Harry H. Pace, president of the biggest black business in Chicago, the Supreme Liberty Life Insurance Company. Pace was also one of the most respected leaders of the black community.

Following the speech, John dashed forward to congratulate Mr. Pace on his fine talk. Pace had obviously heard about the eager young man and asked him what his plans were. John told him about the scholarship he received from the University of Chicago, but added that he still did not have enough money to be able to accept it.

Pace suggested that John try going to school part-time and working part-time, but John explained that he had no luck in finding any kind of job for the fall. Pace hesitated for a moment and then spoke.

"I'm going away on vacation," he said, "but I'll be back in September. See me on the first working day in September and I'll find something for you to do."

Those few moments started John Johnson on what was to become a fantastic career.

Chapter 4

A Supreme Lesson

It took a lot of nerve to walk into the office of the president of Supreme Liberty Life Insurance Company (now called Supreme Life) and tell the secretary that Mr. Pace was expecting him. But the newly named John Johnson had prepared himself well for this September day in 1936.

Though only eighteen years old, John knew that you *never* go into a man's office looking for a job unless you know something about his background, his business, his interests, and his hobbies. John knew that Pace was an author, lawyer, **entrepreneur,** and interested in promoting black entertainers. He had the first black-owned recording company; discovered the singer, Ethel Waters; and was the first person to bring the work of W.C. Handy, a musician and blues composer, to national attention. Pace was also interested in black causes as well as in encouraging talented black people who came his way, from Paul Robeson, the great singer, to Walter White, the leader of the National Association for the Advancement of Colored People (NAACP).

THE "GO-FER"

Although there was no real job waiting for John at Supreme Liberty, Pace assigned him to a desk outside his office. For the first few months John was a "go-fer" – assigned to going on errands for others. But John did not waste the time. Here was a firsthand opportunity to observe a **corporation** – a *black* corporation – with clerks, salesmen, people who managed money and made important business decisions. Working part-time at Supreme Liberty, John received twenty-five dollars a month and managed to attend the University of Chicago part-time, hoping to obtain a law degree.

But the pull of business at Supreme Liberty was so great that John soon dropped out of the University of Chicago and devoted all his time to his work at the insurance company. He would later take several courses at Northwestern University, in Evanston, Illinois, but his major education during the next five years was gained through his corporate experiences.

Today, John Johnson would not recommend such a course for an ambitious person. In modern society, where so much **technological** knowledge is required, Johnson believes a college degree is a necessity. But in the middle of a depression, when it was difficult for even college-educated people to find work, the job at Supreme Liberty was a real plum.

One day, John decided to slip out of the office to get a soda in a nearby drugstore. *That* was the day Pace called and asked John to come into his office. On John's return, Pace scolded him. "Young man, one thing you've got to learn. I'm paying you to sit at your desk, and you should stay there, even if I *never* call you."

A REAL JOB

John must have remembered the lesson well, for after a few months on the job he became assistant to the editor of the company's monthly newspaper, *The Guardian.* Since writing was one of Pace's loves, he was the editor. Three or four months later, John became assistant editor and by 1939, he was editor of the paper.

One of the benefits of his new position was that John was expected to write about the six men who made up the company's **executive committee.** To do this, he had to get to know about them and their work, which gave John a close-up view of how a corporation operates. He had a golden opportunity to ask questions and to learn procedures, and he made the most of it.

Learning on the Job

Along the way, John learned several lessons that have served him well.

1. Organize your time. Ration it and focus on the most important activities. Do not let other people interfere with your plans, if at all possible.

2. Look at every situation and determine its importance

to you. If it fits in with your plans and ambitions, give it your full attention. If not, do not waste time and energy on it.

3. If you assign tasks to others, be sure to check their work to make sure they are keeping with the goals you have set. (In his early years, John learned the hard way about this. He would assign work to others and tell them to have it ready at some future date. John soon realized that if he did not check regularly, the work was delayed or incomplete.)

4. When you need to make a decision, ask yourself, "Will this help me or will this get me in any trouble?" John always felt the second part of the question was the most important.

PLAYING POLITICS

Supreme Liberty was more than just a business. The members of the executive committee were leaders of the black community and were involved in many of the political issues of the day. One who played a large part in the political and legal scene was the top lawyer for Supreme Liberty, Earl B. Dickerson. In an impressive performance before the United States Supreme Court, Dickerson was able to obtain a decision that made it too costly for whites to enforce agreements restricting the sale of property to blacks. Following the Supreme Court's decision, blacks could now buy property in new areas formerly denied to them.

Dickerson also saw the wave of the future in Chicago politics. He was himself a Democrat, and he hoped that by running for the City Council he could bring blacks into the party and break the hold of Mayor Edward J. Kelly's political machine. His opponent in the Second Ward, which was the area of the city in which Dickerson lived, would be a black Republican, William L. Dawson, who was already an alderman (a member of the City Council). Certainly the time was ripe, for in the 1936 presidential election, tens of thousands of black voters went from the Republican to the Democratic Party to vote for Franklin D. Roosevelt.

Suddenly, Johnson found himself in the middle of the political campaign. Pace asked him to help Dickerson by writing news releases. The job soon became far more than that. Johnson realized that whoever saw the candidate last at night was given instructions for the next day's work. Since Johnson was single, had the time, and offered to take on additional assignments, he soon began driving the candidate home at night and picking him up first thing in the morning. In no time, Johnson became Dickerson's chief assistant.

When Dickerson won the election, he named Johnson to the important position of political secretary, a pretty heady job for a person only twenty-one years old. Johnson was excited at the possibility of rising in Chicago politics. But he learned quickly how politics was really played!

Switching Parties: A New Game

The defeated Mr. Dawson switched to the Democratic Party and began working alongside Mayor Kelly. Kelly was more than happy to take on Dawson because the white political machine feared Dickerson's independence. Kelly played it smart by telling blacks that both races should work together to fight their common enemies – unemployment and **racism.**

Dickerson reluctantly agreed to work together, but Kelly undercut Dickerson's power by naming Dawson as a committeeman for the Second Ward. As such, Dawson would take care of ward problems and work with the **precinct captains.** Since most of the contact that the local people had with politicians was through the precinct captains and the ward committeeman, Dawson became the key person in the Second Ward. He helped the local people with their problems and granted favors when they were needed.

Through his work on the City Council, Dickerson tried to rid Chicago of racism. He also was appointed by President Franklin D. Roosevelt to the first Fair Employment Practices Committee (FEPC). This committee marked the beginning of the federal government's efforts to help improve economic conditions for blacks. Dickerson, however, used his position on the committee to attack both the mayor of Chicago and the administration in Washington. He became such a nuisance on the FEPC that Roosevelt was forced to reorganize the committee to get rid of him.

In the next aldermanic election, Dawson regained his seat in the City Council by charging Dickerson with being a "silk stocking" (rich) liberal, uninterested in the problems of the local people. Dawson went on to become a power in Chicago politics and enjoyed a long career in the United States Congress.

Though he was greatly disappointed with the election results, Johnson concluded that the blacks needed both types of men in politics. They needed Dawson's day-by-day assistance to the local people, but they also needed Dickerson's outspoken courage and vision for the future. Johnson remained friendly with both men until their deaths.

FINDING A LIFETIME PARTNER

By 1939, the nation's economy was recovering. The beginning of World War II in Europe created new war industries and new jobs in the United States. John Johnson was earning $50 a week at Supreme Liberty and an additional $50 as Dickerson's political secretary. For the first time, he could afford a car, a light-brown Chevrolet, and to date young women.

In 1940, Johnson met Eunice Walker at a dance. She was a student at Talladega College, in Talladega, Alabama, and was vacationing in Chicago. John had come to the dance with another woman, and Eunice was there with her date. But when they were introduced, something special erupted between them.

Fortunately, after her graduation from Talladega, Eunice returned to Chicago to take a master's degree in social work at Loyola University, and the affection she and John had felt initially had a chance to grow. John found her to be a wonderful listener, who understood his ambitions and believed in him.

But John was hardly a great marriage prospect for a young woman who came from one of the most important black families in the South. Her father was a doctor in Selma, Alabama, and her mother's father, Dr. William H. Alpine, was one of the founders of Selma University and the National Baptist Convention.

John's persistence paid off, however, and the couple were married in Selma on June 21, 1941. Eunice took the train home while John drove to Selma in a new red car. John could not afford a traditional honeymoon, so the ride back to Chicago and a visit to a friend in Atlanta, Georgia, served as their honeymoon. They began married life in a three-room apartment in South Chicago. It was the first of many homes in their climb to success.

Chapter 5

A Capital Idea

Pearl Harbor. The United States entry into World War II. The **Jim Crow** draft. Once again, as in World War I, blacks and whites were being asked to serve their country. And once again, the blacks were called to serve in "black only" units. In some cases, black troops were forced to eat in the kitchen at some southern railway stations, while German prisoners of war traveling on the same train ate in the dining car. Blacks, even **conservatives** like William Dawson, were calling for an end to racism, in defense industries and in the draft.

John Johnson was one of the many blacks who signed up at the draft board on 55th Street in Chicago, but he was fortunate enough to be number 3,990 in a lottery of 4,000 registrants. For the moment, he could go on with his work at Supreme Liberty.

EMPLOYEE UNREST

But the war and the new "black awareness" were even affecting work at the insurance company. **Employees** were beginning to demand labor reforms, and their target became Harry Pace, the president of Supreme Liberty.

Pace was a black who was so fair-skinned that he could easily have passed as a white man. Many blacks merely wink and smile when a black begins passing as white, but others become angry at what they see as a rejection of the black race. During the early months of the war, Pace moved to a white suburb where, it was rumored, his children were passing as whites. Angry employees at Supreme Liberty threatened to demonstrate in front of Pace's suburban home in order to embarrass him. Johnson could not side with the plan and warned Pace about it. Pace left his car in front of the building and escaped through the rear, foiling the plan because the employees thought he was still in his office. From that day on, Pace became more secretive about his movements and even stopped carrying home black newspapers and magazines.

GETTING STARTED ON HIS OWN

Pace's problem indirectly provided Johnson with his first chance at being an entrepreneur. Pace now felt that he was getting old and he asked Johnson to take on a new task. Would John read newspapers and magazines in order to find out what was happening in the black world and write a digest, or summary, of events?

Johnson was excited with the new project and thoroughly enjoyed the research he needed to do in order to prepare the digests. He soon became the center of attention at social gatherings as he told about the many things going on in the black world.

At that time, there was hardly any information in the white press about events going on in black communities. The only time a black's picture was printed in a newspaper was when he committed a crime. The marriages, births, and deaths of blacks – none of these appeared in white newspapers until the 1960s.

The Dawn of a Fresh Idea

It suddenly dawned on Johnson that people were tremendously interested in his stories about the achievements and hopes of blacks. Perhaps he could start a magazine like *Reader's Digest* or *Time* that would be dedicated to black events.

Johnson's first attempts proved useless. No black businessman was willing to **invest** in the project or offer any encouragement. He even went to New York to speak with Roy Wilkins, who edited *The Crisis*, the magazine of the NAACP. Wilkins told John to save his energy and his money. Years later, when Wilkins had become executive director of the NAACP, he admitted his mistake. It was one of the sweetest moments in Johnson's life.

Using His Own Assets

But John was not about to give up. He reflected on one of his own rules and asked himself, "What can I do by myself with what I have in order to get what I want?" He soon realized that he had three **assets.**

First, he had a mailing list – the list of customers of Supreme Liberty. Second, one of his less important jobs at Supreme was to run the addressing machine. And third, when he asked Pace about the possibility of using both the mailing list and the machine, Pace gave him permission.

Johnson decided to send a letter to Supreme's 20,000 customers asking for two dollars for a prepaid **subscription** to a new magazine. He figured that if only fifteen percent of the people responded, he would have $6,000, enough to publish the first issue of his magazine. But there was still one more problem. John needed $500, a large sum of money in those days, to buy stamps to mail the letters.

Bucking the Bankers

In desperation, Johnson went to the First National Bank of Chicago to ask for a loan. He was told by an assistant to an assistant, "Boy, we don't make any loans to colored people." (Today, Johnson Publications is one of First National's most prized customers, with an open line of credit.)

John remembered the advice in the self-help books he had read: "Don't get mad. Get smart." He asked the assistant if there was any place where a black might get a loan, and he was referred to the Citizens Loan Corporation. At Citizens Loan he was told he could have a loan if he had collateral.

"What do you mean by collateral?" John asked.

He was told that if he had a house or furniture, he could pledge that as a guarantee that he would pay the loan. If he failed to repay, of course, the house or furniture would be taken by the bank.

Mother Comes to the Rescue

The only furniture John could think of as collateral was the new pieces he had recently helped his mother buy. But Gertrude was not eager to lose the furniture she had saved so long to purchase.

"I'll have to consult the Lord about this," she said. Day after day, John asked his mother for an answer, and all she would say was, "I'm still praying." After four days, he said, "Maybe, I'd better pray with you."

At last, Gertrude agreed that the Lord wanted her to put up the furniture as collateral. John immediately delivered to the bank a paper showing that the furniture was all paid for. He now had a check for $500.

Giving the Customer What He Wants

John's next task was to write the kind of letter that would spark the interest of the reader enough to make him part with two dollars. In the back of his mind was what he had learned about salesmanship: *Ask not what you want but what the customer or the potential customer wants.*

Marketing a New Product

It is not enough for an entrepreneur to have a good idea for a product. To be successful, he must be able to market his product. He must study the demographics, to determine the number of people who might be interested in his product, the ages of the people who might buy it, and where they are located. It is also important to know what income is needed for the **consumer** to afford the product.

Other factors may also have to be considered. In the case of beginning a new magazine, the publisher will want to know the level of literacy, reading ability, or education that the consumer will need. It may also be important to know what the average reader's interests are. Is the magazine aimed at a reader interested in sports, politics, or cultural events like theater, music, and movies?

It was advice John would later give to job applicants who came in explaining how much they needed a job and how much it would mean to them. The right approach is to learn as much as one can about the company and tell the possible future employer what you have to offer to help the company.

To this day, Johnson remembers the letter, which read:

Dear Mr. Brown:

A good friend of yours told me about you.

He told me that you are a person who likes to keep abreast of local and national events.

He said you are the kind of person who will be interested in a magazine that will help you become more knowledgeable about your own people and about what they are doing to win greater recognition for you and other members of our race. Because of your position in the community and the recommendation I received, I would like to offer you a reduced rate on the magazine *Negro Digest,* which will be published in the next thirty days. Magazine subscriptions will sell for $3.00 a year, but in view of the recommendation we are offering a subscription to you for $2.00, if you send your check or money order by September 30.

John had received permission from Earl Dickerson to use a small section of the law library in the Supreme Liberty building as an office and mailing address. This became the first office of the *Negro Digest.* Three thousand people responded to the letters, enough for the first printing.

Meantime, John was working desperately to get permission to reprint articles from black newspapers and white magazines. He would work in the Supreme offices during the day and on the magazine at night. Eunice, who was working as a social worker during the day, would help at night. Other friends also helped.

The next hurdle was to have the magazine printed. One of John's tasks at Supreme Liberty was to work with the Progress Printing Company, which did printing for the insurance company. When John strolled in and told the printer, "We were thinking about publishing a magazine," the printer assumed that

Supreme was behind the **venture** and did not question how the bill would be paid.

On November 1, 1942, the first 5,000 copies of *Negro Digest* rolled off the presses. It contained sixty-eight pages and included material written by famous authors and noted clergymen, both black and white. Not one white publication noted the arrival of the new magazine, but it was mentioned in a few black newspapers.

Determining the Selling Price

If a new product will be competing with other similar products, the entrepreneur will want to know what the competition is offering, its selling price, and how it differs from or resembles his new product. Knowing these factors will help the entrepreneur determine what to charge for the new item.

If a new magazine, for example, has more pages, higher quality paper, and is aimed at a wealthier consumer than any other magazine, the price may be higher. On the other hand, if it is to be smaller in size, with fewer pages, it may be necessary to charge less. In any event, the selling price must be sufficient for the entrepreneur to make a reasonable profit after paying all his costs of production, overhead, advertising, and distribution.

SELLING AN IDEA

The next job was to see that people bought the magazine. Three thousand copies were sent to the original subscribers, but how was John going to sell the other 2,000? He had to find some company that would distribute his magazine, get it out on news-stands all over the city. So he used the Yellow Pages in the telephone book, which has a listing of companies under a variety of categories.

Distribution and Advertising

There are several ways a product can be introduced or marketed to the public. One is by in-store demonstrations and displays. That is often done with new kitchen gadgets or cosmetics. New foods or household products are often demonstrated in local supermarkets. A new magazine may be displayed at check-out counters so customers will look at it as they wait to go through a line.

Advertising in magazines, newspapers, radio, and television is a very popular way to introduce a new product. For some products, like insurance, there may be telephone solicitations, direct phone calls to a potential customer's home.

John prepared himself, as usual, and visited the biggest **distributor** in Chicago, the Charles Levy Circulating Company. In an interview with Joseph Levy, brother of the company's founder, John gave all the reasons why the company should take on this new publication.

Levy's reply was, "We don't handle colored books."

John's first reaction was anger, but he controlled himself and asked quietly, "Is that because you're prejudiced or because colored books don't sell?"

"Johnson," retorted Joseph Levy, "I'm Jewish – I don't believe in prejudice. It's because colored books don't sell."

It was now John Johnson's turn to prove that his magazine *would* sell. And the only way he could do that was to get people to buy the magazine. He returned to the Supreme office and asked thirty of his friends to go to the Levy newsstands and ask for a copy of the *Negro Digest.* The plan worked!

The Distribution Problem Solved

Levy called Johnson and admitted that he had received requests for the magazine. Would Johnson send him 500 copies? Johnson rushed to the Levy office and convinced Joseph Levy that he should take 1,000 copies. But now John had to send his friends all over town to buy up the copies of the magazine. Taking the last bit of money that he had, John paid his friends to purchase the magazine. Levy responded by ordering another 1,000 copies.

The news was out. Newsstand vendors would ask black customers, "Have you seen the new magazine, *Negro Digest?*" More and more black people began to pick up copies of the publication. Johnson rushed through another printing of 5,000 copies. The magazine had been successfully launched!

Spreading the Word

Levy became one of Johnson's most enthusiastic supporters. He not only offered suggestions for **marketing** the magazine, he put posters on the sides of his trucks advertising the new publication. Levy also helped John make connections with white distributors in New York, Detroit, and other big cities. Johnson returned the favor by helping Levy break into the distribution system of the close-knit black community.

Johnson also used black distributors throughout the country and hired other people by running ads in black newspapers. Postal workers who knew the city and worked at night were willing to sell the magazine during the day. Many of the people did not have the money to buy the magazines in advance, so Johnson set up **accounts** for them in several cities. They would get the magazines, put the earnings in a special Negro Digest Publishing Company account, and thus have money to buy future copies of the magazine. Money could be deposited into but not removed from the accounts. From time to time, Johnson would transfer the money to the Chicago office.

Prejudice and Pressure

In the South, however, the story was quite different. Sheriffs and police chiefs strongly opposed the distribution of any black publications. So sellers of the magazine had to use different tactics. They boarded buses and streetcars to sell copies. They also went out to the cotton fields and sold them. Not even beatings or jail stopped their determination.

When Johnson Publishing Company celebrated its 40th birthday, special tribute was paid to the men and women of the South who had endured so much to get the magazines to a waiting black public.

Chapter 6

The Birth of Ebony

No doubt about it. *Negro Digest* was a fantastic success. After eight months, **circulation** reached 50,000. For almost a year, John Johnson continued to work at Supreme Liberty while publishing his magazine with the help of Eunice and several friends. But he did not have one full-time employee. In order to make the magazine look as if it were being published by a large and successful corporation, John listed on the **masthead** his friend, Ben Burns, a **free-lance** writer, as associate editor. Also listed on the masthead was E.M. Walker, his wife's maiden name, and G.J. Williams, his mother's name.

THE PRESIDENT'S WIFE TO THE RESCUE

For a while, the magazine's circulation stayed at 50,000 copies per issue. But Johnson knew that, as with any business, the magazine had to grow. If one stands still, the business is apt to decline. He needed something to generate publicity and increase sales.

One of John's successful regular features in the magazine was a column entitled "If I Were a Negro." In this column, well-known whites were asked to respond to such questions as: "Would you be willing to wait another generation for quality education for your children?" or "Would you want your sons and fathers and brothers to fight . . . in a **segregated** army?"

Johnson decided that the person he most wanted to write for his magazine was Eleanor Roosevelt, the wife of the President. She was a liberal and warm person, who was constantly being denounced in the press for meeting with blacks. Remembering his mother's advice, John sat down and wrote a letter to Mrs. Roosevelt. She replied that she would like to help, but she didn't have the time. But Johnson persisted, and when he learned that Mrs. Roosevelt was coming to Chicago, he sent a telegram to her hotel after she had arrived. Almost immediately he received an article written exclusively for his magazine.

On visiting the offices of *Negro Digest* later, Mrs. Roosevelt explained that she had finished her own work early and the telegram arrived just as she had a little time to herself. The article that Mrs. Roosevelt wrote that day explained that if she were black, she would have great bitterness *and* great patience.

Southern white newspapers jumped on Mrs. Roosevelt's comments about being patient, and newspapers in the North picked up the part about bitterness. Almost overnight, the circulation of *Negro Digest* jumped from 50,000 to 100,000.

MOVING UP

Within the year, John Johnson was making more money than he had ever dreamed of. Still feeling that the bubble might burst, John asked for a leave of absence from Supreme Liberty rather than making a clean break with the company. That leave lasted for twenty years, until Johnson returned to take over control of the insurance company.

To John's surprise, he found that the more money he made, the more he had to give to the government. He hired a brilliant young black **accountant,** Charles A. Beckett, who suggested that John invest in properties, some of which would lose money and offset the **profits** he was making in his publishing company. Though it sounded crazy to Johnson, it is one of the **loopholes** that the government often provides that allows wealthy people to keep a larger share of their money.

John now bought his first office building and his first home, a three-story apartment building. Eunice and John lived on the first floor, his mother and stepfather lived on the second. Shortly after, John told his mother that she would never again have to work. From that day in 1943 until she died, she had a car, a chauffeur, a maid, and money enough to travel anywhere she wished.

TAKING ADVICE FROM THOSE IN THE KNOW

John now had a growing staff and the business was flourishing. But he recognized that he did not know much about magazine publishing, advertising, or organizing a circulation department. However, he was never embarrassed to seek advice from those who knew more than he did. Whenever possible, he went straight to the top.

John would call a company, announce that he was the president of his own company, and ask to speak to the president of the concern he was calling. In speaking to the secretary of Henry Luce, head of the company that published *Time* and *Life* magazines, John said, "If the president of the smallest country in the world comes to Washington, our president . . . will see him. So it seems to me that your president, in the American tradition, will see me."

Henry Luce did meet John and made arrangements for him to talk to all kinds of experts in the *Time-Life* organization. Other famous people liked Johnson's approach and were also willing to share their knowledge.

THE WAR HITS NEGRO DIGEST

No business runs smoothly, especially when there's a war going on. John Johnson had little time to savor his success. In April 1945, the government notified him that in order to meet the demands of war, he would have to reduce the amount of paper he used for his magazines. But John knew that if he cut back on paper, he would have to cut down his circulation. He would be ruined.

Johnson decided to seek the help of a lawyer, J. Norman Goddess. The advice that Goddess gave him was to go to Washington *without* a lawyer and plead his own case. What

Goddess was suggesting was that Johnson would do better to pretend to be a poor black who knew nothing about complicated government laws.

John did just that. He prepared his plea carefully and appeared alone before the War Production Board. Of the twenty-five people who came before the Board on that day, Johnson was the only one who did not have a lawyer. And his case was the only one that was approved.

A NEW MAGAZINE

For some time, two of Johnson's most dedicated free-lancers, Ben Burns, a white journalist, and Jay Jackson, an art editor, had been pestering Johnson to try a new venture. They wanted to create a new magazine called *Jive,* which would focus on the black music and entertainment world. In order to keep the two men happy, Johnson agreed to a three-way partnership. Each of the partners would put up $1,000 and share the profits three ways. But when the time came for Burns and Jackson to pay their shares, they were unable to do so.

Rather than let the matter drop, Johnson suggested a new deal. The year was 1945. World War II was almost over. The time was ripe for a new magazine, but *not* the kind that Burns and Jackson had suggested. Johnson would raise the pay that the two men had been receiving and he would create a new magazine along some ideas he had. Since Johnson was investing all the money, all profits, would, of course, go to him. The agreement satisfied all three men.

Pictures and Black Achievement

Johnson was convinced that the wave of the future was going to be picture magazines, like Henry Luce's highly successful *Life*. Television had not yet arrived, but Johnson was sure that what the black public wanted was a magazine that had glamour and would show pictures of high-achieving blacks. His magazine would feature people like Jackie Robinson, the first black to break into major league baseball, and Dr. Ralph Bunche, a black who would later win the Nobel Peace Prize.

And because the white press never wrote about black births, weddings, or debutante balls, Johnson was determined to show that there was a black society that had its own glamour and held charity events. Johnson also made it clear that the issue of race would be openly discussed in his new magazine.

It was Eunice Johnson who suggested the name *Ebony* for the new magazine. It is the name of a fine, hard, black tree in Africa. The word came to symbolize black pride and accomplishment.

Negro Digest had hardly been noticed by the white press. Now it was different. *Time* and *Newsweek* were among the many publications that wrote about the newest arrival, *Ebony*. Within a few months following its first publication in November 1945, the magazine's staff had expanded far beyond the three originators, and Johnson had to rent a two-story building to house his growing staff. Almost immediately, *Ebony* became the biggest black magazine in both size and circulation. It holds that title even today.

CIRCULATION ISN'T ENOUGH

The first issue of *Ebony* did not carry a single ad. Johnson had decided that until he could guarantee advertisers a circulation of 100,000 readers, he would not go out to seek any advertising. But after just six months, Johnson could make that guarantee. However, he still had a problem. He could not find

Overhead, Labor, and Other Costs

There are precise costs that must be considered when deciding the selling price of a new item or service. What is the actual cost of printing a magazine, for example? What does the printer charge for 50,000 copies, for 100,000 copies, for 500,000 copies? Usually, the greater the number of copies printed, the less the cost per copy. That is true of most products.

What is the cost of labor—the salaries of people who work on the magazine such as the writers, editors, and the office staff? In addition, one must consider overhead. This includes such costs as light, heat, telephone, cleaning services for the offices, insurance, and rental or mortgage costs for the building or manufacturing plant.

enough advertisers to support the high cost of producing a magazine that used high-quality paper and was filled with expensive photographs.

The cost of producing magazines and newspapers can never be paid for by newsstand sales alone. Money must also be brought in by advertising. The more copies of *Ebony* that Johnson sold, the more money he was losing. He had to convince white companies to advertise in the magazine. For one solid year, John Johnson spent almost every waking hour trying to sell this idea.

Zenith Signs Up

Johnson finally hit on the idea of trying to reach a company that had a large following in the black community. Almost all blacks owned radios, the most popular of which was Zenith. A letter to Commander Eugene McDonald, head of Zenith, brought only the response that he did not handle advertising, only company **policy.** Johnson wrote McDonald another letter stating that he would like to discuss company advertising policy. McDonald agreed to see him, but warned him not to try to sell advertising at their meeting.

Johnson prepared himself well for that meeting. He looked up McDonald in *Who's Who in America* and discovered that he had been an Arctic explorer who had been to the North Pole after it had been reached by Commodore Robert E. Peary and by a black man, Matt Henson. Henson had written a book about his experiences. Johnson obtained a copy of the book, autographed by Henson, for McDonald.

Johnson also included a four-page story about Matt Henson in the July 1947 issue of *Ebony*. So when McDonald began the meeting by talking about Matt Henson, Johnson was well prepared. McDonald loved the personally autographed copy of Henson's book, and he was impressed with the magazine article Johnson showed him.

By the end of the meeting, McDonald called in his advertising manager and suggested strongly that Zenith products should be advertised in *Ebony*. McDonald also called the **chairman** of several other major corporations and suggested that they meet with Johnson. They did, and all eventually bought ads. *Ebony's* survival was assured. In 1971, Johnson became a member of the Zenith **Board of Directors.**

WHAT WORKED YESTERDAY

In one sense, it was hard to see *Ebony* outstrip *Negro Digest*. The *Digest* had been Johnson's first love, his first success. He waited six years before he took steps to discontinue publishing the magazine. But he knew only too well that he had to move ahead.

Too often, businessmen lose out because of what Johnson calls "the fatal disease, 'WWY' " – what worked yesterday. He learned early on that a businessman must change with the times. He must anticipate what the customer wants and plan to fulfill that need. He must get out of his office, observe the consumer in shops and markets, and give the customer the right product.

In the 1960s, Johnson saw a need for a magazine to promote the works of black writers and artists, and to meet the need of those blacks who wanted more than entertainment in their reading matter. In keeping with the times, he began publication of a new magazine called *Black World*. But when the freedom movement of the '60s faded, *Black World's* circulation went from 100,000 to 15,000 and, as he did with *Negro Digest*, Johnson dropped the magazine. But by this time, Johnson was also publishing other magazines: *Jet, Tan,* and *Hue*.

Chapter 7

Rebirth of the Black Spirit and National Recognition

The ten years following the birth of *Ebony* in November 1945 also saw the beginning of major changes for blacks in America. The Supreme Court banned segregation in public schools, segregation in the armed forces was ended, and decisions by federal courts increased the number of blacks going to the polls to vote. And Dr. Martin Luther King, Jr., began his famous **boycott** of the buses in Montgomery, Alabama.

When Dr. King called a Morehouse College classmate, Robert E. Johnson, for help in spreading news about the rising freedom movement, Robert Johnson relayed the message

John Johnson, third from right, and Mrs. Johnson at the 100th anniversary celebration of the Emancipation Proclamation in 1963. Seated in the front row are Ethel Kennedy (left), Vice-president and Mrs. Lyndon Johnson, and President and Mrs. John Kennedy (John F. Kennedy Library.)

to John Johnson. Robert was told to get the next plane south. *Ebony* and *Jet* now became leading voices in the black fight for equality.

TWO KINDS OF LEADERS

The 1960s were marked by a rebirth of the black spirit and the emergence of John Johnson as a national black leader. While Martin Luther King fought for the **civil rights** movement in Alabama and in Washington, D.C., John Johnson led a different kind of battle. He struggled for economic equality for black businessmen and for an appreciation of blacks as an important part of the consumer market.

Johnson's goal was to make white business corporations aware that blacks had income to spend, that they would buy advertised products if they are appealed to directly. At that time, there were no black advertising agencies or black fashion models in advertisements. Johnson personally visited the major corporations. He went back time after time to sell the idea that advertising in a black magazine would open up a whole new market for their products. As always, he arrived well prepared with business figures and strong arguments. In time, his efforts paid off.

Not only did Johnson obtain advertisements from such major companies as Chrysler Corporation and Sears Roebuck, he ended up being asked to serve as a member of the board of directors of some of the most important companies in the country. Today, blacks are regularly featured in magazines, newspaper, and television commercials.

SUCCESS BREEDS SUCCESS

Johnson also took every opportunity to create new businesses. In 1951, his second most successful magazine, *Jet,* hit the newsstands. Within six months, it became the largest black news magazine in the world. In 1958, Johnson was asked to locate some black models for a fashion show for Ernestine Dent, wife of the president of Dillard University, in New Orleans. He promptly offered to put on the fashion show for her. This fashion show eventually became the *Ebony* Fashion Show, directed by Johnson's wife, Eunice. Every year, Eunice and Linda, Johnson's daughter, travel to the great fashion houses in Europe to buy clothes for these shows. Through their efforts, more than twenty-five million dollars have been raised for black charities.

In 1973, Johnson branched out to a new industry with the purchase of a Chicago radio station, WJPC. By 1984, the Johnson Publishing Company had edged out a record company, Motown Productions, to become the top corporation on a list of the 100 largest black-owned businesses in the United States.

In 1974, Fashion Fair Cosmetics was founded. Noting that black fashion models often had to mix their own colors to obtain the right shades of cosmetics, Johnson sought help from white cosmetics firms. He asked several of the major cosmetic companies to create new shades for the black consumer. None of them was interested. So John and Eunice asked a private laboratory to design a new line of products especially for black women. He used many of the same tactics to obtain acceptance for his new products as he had used years before to introduce *Negro Digest.*

AN AVALANCHE OF HONORS

John Johnson received his first national award in 1951, when he was chosen as one of the country's Ten Outstanding Young Men by the United States Junior Chamber of Commerce. In 1966, he received the Spingarn Medal from the National Association for the Advancement of Colored People for the "highest and noblest achievement by an American Negro during the preceding year or years." That same year, he was one of twelve Americans to win the Horatio Alger Award, which is given annually by the American Schools and Colleges Association to "living individuals who by their own efforts have

President Ronald Reagan greeting John Johnson at a dinner in the White House in honor of Mikhail Gorbachev, General Secretary of the Soviet Union (far left). (National Archives.)

Eunice and John Johnson with the Prime Minister of England, Margaret Thatcher, at President Reagan's last official dinner at the White House. (National Archives.)

pulled themselves up by their bootstraps in the American tradition."

MEETING PRESIDENT EISENHOWER

By the mid-1950s, Johnson's name was known well enough to open corporate doors all over the United States – and to be invited to the White House by President Dwight D. (Ike) Eisenhower. Once there, Johnson soon realized why he had been invited.

Johnson explains this in his autobiography, *Succeeding Against the Odds.* "The Republicans didn't have much Black support and *Ebony* was, by then, the most powerful communicator in Black America. From Ike on, every U.S. president communicated with me because *Ebony* communicated so well with Black Americans."

During the turbulent days of the 1960s, when civil rights marches were at their height, Johnson became an unofficial black **ambassador** to the white corporate world. Time after time, he was asked to make speeches at company meetings or to meet with top executives, who wished to understand what was happening in black America.

John and Eunice Johnson's names are high on the list of invitations to the White House when foreign visitors are expected. Through such dinners, the Johnsons have met Prime Minister Golda Meir of Israel, President Mikhail Gorbachev of the Soviet Union, and Prime Minister Margaret Thatcher of England.

Chapter 8

The Rewards of Success

John Johnson is the most successful black entrepreneur in American history. In 1982, he was listed by *Forbes* magazine as one of the 400 richest Americans, with a net worth of over 100 million dollars. Today, he owns a beautiful home perched on a mountainside in Palm Springs, California. His neighbor is Bob Hope. He also owns a magnificent apartment in Chicago.

One of John's dreams had been to create a showplace building for the Johnson Publishing Company. This was achieved with the grand opening of an eleven-story office building in 1972. The mayor of Chicago, Richard Daley, spoke at the event, and Gwendolyn Brooks, a Pulitzer Prize-winning poet, read a poem she had written specially for the occasion.

In 1974, Johnson was elected chairman and chief executive officer (CEO) of Supreme Life Insurance Company, the company in which he had started years before as an office

54

boy. He would later be asked to serve on the board of directors of the Chrysler Corporation, the Continental Bank, and Twentieth Century Fox, a motion picture company.

In 1975, Harvard University celebrated John H. Johnson Day, the first black businessman to be so honored. Many more honors and awards would be given to the publisher in the following years.

THE QUALITY OF LOVE

For all his success, there were things in John Johnson's life over which he had no control. One was the great sadness that he experienced when his beloved mother and his son died.

In 1965, John and Eunice adopted a little boy. They named him John Harold, Jr. Two years later, they adopted a daughter, Linda. Johnson was an adoring father and Eunice insisted on taking care of the children herself, despite the fact that they could well afford a nurse.

But when only two years old, John Jr. became ill with sickle-cell anemia. It is a fatal, chronic, hereditary blood disease found primarily in Africans or persons of African descent. John Jr. went through periods of health and severe illness, and the family suffered with him. Most sickle-cell patients die in their teens. But because he had such good medical care and the help of his family, John Jr. survived a little longer. He died at age twenty-five. In memory of their son, the Johnsons gave a waiting room with the latest emergency equipment to Wyler Children's Hospital, in Chicago.

The loss of his mother was also one of the saddest days

John Johnson with his daughter, Linda Johnson Rice, now the president of Johnson Publishing Company, which, with annual revenues of $250 million, is the second-largest black business in the country. (Jonathan Kirn/NYT Pictures.)

of John Johnson's life. Gertrude had been his most ardent supporter. She had made possible the $500 loan that enabled him to start his first magazine, and she had been there to encourage him whenever things seemed at their worst. On the sixth floor of the Johnson Publishing Company Building, Gertrude's office, exactly as she left it, remains as a memorial to her spirit.

CARRYING ON IN THE FUTURE

By the time Linda was seven years old, she began joining her mother on yearly trips to the fashion capitals of Europe to buy clothes for Eunice's fashion shows. But Linda wanted more than a career in the fashion world. She first earned a degree in journalism from the University of Southern California. Then one day she approached her father and asked, "What about training me for your job?"

John Johnson was only too happy to prepare Linda for taking over the business. After receiving her master's degree from Northwestern University, she went to work for her father. Today, Linda is president and chief operating officer of the company.

John Johnson also knows that the future promises another generation to carry on what he began. In November 1984, at a magnificent wedding in Chicago, Linda married Andre Rice, stockbroker. When his first grandchild, Alexa Christina, was born four years later, John Johnson knew that the business he had worked so hard to create and develop would go on.

Glossary

accountant   One skilled in taking care of public or private accounts.

accounts   Records of monies received and paid out.

ambassador   The official highest ranking representative of a foreign government.

assets   The entire property (land, money, talents) of a person or corporation.

board of directors   A group of people entrusted with the responsibility of determining the policies, or guidelines, for the operation of an organization.

boycott   To refuse to do something, such as buy certain products, in order to force acceptance of certain conditions.

chairman   The person who presides over, or runs, a committee or an organization.

circulation   The average number of copies of a newspaper or magazine sold over a given period.

civil rights   The right to full legal, social, and economic equality extended to all citizens of a country.

conservative   One who supports a traditional or existing point of view in politics on social or economic action.

consumer   One who buys or uses economic goods.

corporation   A group of people formed to carry on a business enterprise, with legally given rights and duties.

deposit   Money put into a bank for safekeeping.

depression   A period of low economic activity, marked by much unemployment.

distributor   One who helps to market or sell a product.

economy   The system concerned with the production, distribution, and consumption of goods and services.

employee   People hired to work for other people.

entrepreneur   One who organizes, manages, and assumes the risks of a business.

executive committee   A group of individuals who direct the activities of an organization.

free-lance   To engage in a profession without any long-term contract with an employer.

interest   Money paid for the use of borrowed funds.

invest   To put money into something in order to get a return of more income.

Jim Crow   Anything having to do with discrimination against blacks.

loophole   An omission in a law or contract through which the intent of the law or contract can be evaded legally.

marketing   The advertising and selling of products by companies.

masthead   The part of a newspaper or magazine that gives the names of the publisher and staff.

mortgage   A real estate loan that generally covers an extended number of years.

policy   A definite course of action selected from several alternatives to help guide future decisions.

precinct captain   A political party leader who works for election purposes within a subdivision of a city.

prejudice   An attitude of hostility against an individual, group, or race because of their supposed characteristics.

profits   The extra money made between the cost and the selling price of an item.

racism   A belief that racial differences produce an inherent superiority of a particular race.

relief   Government aid to the poor, aged, or handicapped.

segregate   To separate or set apart one group from the rest of society.

subscription   A signed order for regular delivery of a magazine or newspaper.

technological   Describing the application of scientific knowledge to solve problems, especially in industry and engineering.

venture   A business undertaking that has an element of risk.

Index